VIDYAMALA BURCH

MINDFULNESS OF DAILY LIFE

Contents

Introduction 6
What is Mindfulness? 7

Mindfulness of Activities 9
Aligning your goals with your circumstances 9
How to recognise your values 10
Sustainers and drainers 11
Alice 12
The 'boom-and-bust' cycle 13
Caroline 15
Breaking the cycle 15
You decide how you live, not your pain or your feelings 15
Pacing or 'rhythm' 16
Betty 17

Four Steps to Pacing 17
Present moment awareness 17
Prioritising 17
Planning 18
Jenny 18
Pacing or 'mindfulness rhythm' 18

The Breathworks Mindfulness in Daily Life (Pacing) Programme 19
Keeping a diary 20
Mindfulness of daily activity diary example sheets 21
Analysing your diary 24
Diary extract example sheet 25
Establishing baselines 26
Baseline record example sheet 28
Jenny 29

Three-Minute Breathing Space 30
Janet 31

Mindfulness of Eating and Sleeping 31
Sally 32

Issues in Mindfulness of Daily Life 33
Aren't planning and pacing boring and restrictive? 33
Maria 34
The need for acceptance 34
Doing your best 34
Diane 35
Pacing in Public 35
Activities you can't leave or think you can't pace 36
Pacing with a degenerative condition 36
Bill 37
Sometimes pacing means doing more, not less 37
Steve 38
Do something enjoyable in rest periods 38

Summary 39

Appendix 1:
Physical consequences of reduced activity 41
Appendix 2:
Sense Awareness Inventory 43
Appendix 3:
Diary templates for photocopying 45

Footnotes 56
Vidyamala 57
More from Breathworks 57

Introduction

This booklet is based on my experience of using mindfulness to manage severe chronic back pain for more than 30 years following surgery and a car accident. Twenty years ago, I had the good fortune to come across mindfulness and meditation. Putting these methods into practice has gradually transformed my life. In 2001 I established Breathworks – an organisation offering mindfulness to others suffering pain, illness or stress and my book *Living Well with Pain and Illness* goes into the complete Breathworks approach. I also decided to produce this booklet as an expansion of chapter 17, so people could have a more detailed and systematic introduction in to how to bring mindfulness into the nitty gritty of the everyday.

For many years my main mindfulness practice consisted of a daily meditation practice of 30-40 minutes. Although I found this extremely helpful in terms of bringing about calm and more positive mental and emotional states, I found it impossible to sustain this awareness once I engaged with the normal activities of daily life. All too often I would get more and more strained and exhausted as my habits of over-doing it and trying to push away my pain kicked in during the day. I would end up collapsing on my bed feeling defeated, yet again, by my circumstances.

Eventually I decided to research different approaches to pain and stress management and this booklet is the fruit of my experiments. I drew on approaches to pacing used in Cognitive Behavioural Therapy as well as traditional mindfulness practice and designed the Breathworks step-by-step pacing programme included later in this booklet.

Pacing – or mindfulness 'rhythm' – means bringing awareness to your activities and spacing them through the day to avoid making your pain worse. It means taking a break *before* you need it, so you keep the pain under control and don't need to rest too much. It means making choices based on intelligence and objectivity rather than being driven by the pain. This more balanced approach to life enables you to maintain your activities more consistently and gradually increase your capacity to be active.

As I have begun to master the art of living *with* my pain rather than *against* it throughout my days, I have come to see that the real art of mindfulness involves much more than meditation. It arises when we learn how to take the quality of awareness gained in meditation into the day to day moments of our lives with a sense of purpose, initiative and choice.

What is Mindfulness?

Mindfulness is a special kind of awareness that is attentive and warmly engaged with each moment of life. It helps us live with a sense of possibility and choice, rather than existing on 'autopilot' – being driven by familiar and often unhelpful habits as we drift from one thing to the next. I sometimes call this the billiard-ball approach to life – we are like a billiard ball bouncing from side to side off the cushions on a billiard table. Of course it is tiring and unrewarding to be a victim of circumstances in this way, but we often don't know how to stop our habits and find a new way of being. Mindfulness provides the key. Before you can make conscious choices about how to respond to experience you need to be **aware**, or **mindful**, of what's happening as it occurs. So mindfulness training consists of becoming aware, over and over again. This might sound simple enough, but it is surprisingly difficult to put into practice and this booklet will give you lots of tips about how to bring mindfulness into all the different activities of the day.

The difference between being on autopilot and being mindful is like the difference between being asleep and awake, and mindfulness is sometimes described as *wakefulness* or alertness. Imagine what life would be like if every moment you continually felt alert, alive and awake — wise, clear, receptive and able to engage with and appreciate the world around you.

Put simply, we could describe mindfulness as: *living in the moment, noticing what is happening and making choices as to how we respond to our experience, rather than being driven by habitual reactions.* Jon Kabat-Zinn, an American mindfulness teacher, describes it as: *'a particular way of paying attention: on purpose, in the present moment, and non-judgmentally.'*[1] He and his colleagues draw out three key aspects:

- Mindfulness is *intentional.* It includes a sense of purpose that enables you to make choices and act with awareness, helping life to unfold in a creative way.
- Mindfulness is *experiential,* focusing on present moment awareness that's based on accurate and direct perception.
- Mindfulness is *non-judgmental.* It allows you to see things as they actually are in the present moment without making harsh value judgements. We definitely need intelligent discernment of our experience just to make our way through the day. But it's important to distinguish this from the 'habit of judging that winds up functioning as an irrational tyrant that can never be satisfied'.[2]

Mindfulness also includes a rich emotional awareness, and it could equally be described as 'heartfulness',[3] or compassionate and kindly awareness. Mind and heart are two doorways into the experience of awareness and both are gradually transformed as your practice of mindfulness deepens. I like to describe mindfulness as *becoming intimate with experience*. If you're caring for a loved one, or a child, it isn't enough to pay attention in a cold and clinical way. With mindfulness our relationship to our impulses and responses includes love, care, tenderness and interest. That means deeply inhabiting the richness of the moment in an embodied and authentic way, which is especially important if you're in pain. You can only look at life with honesty and integrity and be open to its painful and pleasurable sides if you have a soft and open heart, and it takes courage to face the demon of pain instead of frantically running away from it.

Mindfulness of Activities

Aligning your goals with your circumstances

You will only be able to achieve mindfulness in daily life if your goals – what you set out to achieve – are aligned with a realistic sense of your circumstances. This is one of the most crucial and difficult aspects of mindfulness training and it will take you time to gradually orient your whole life in a direction that has meaning for you and yet is also realistic. When I was first living with pain I would repeatedly behave in ways that made my pain worse.

My lack of acceptance and frustration meant that I would still try to do things like move furniture, carry heavy shopping, climb mountains or sit at my computer for hours at a time. Day after day I would end up feeling wrecked and think: *"If only I could get to the point where I no longer want to do the things that harm me."* At the time it seemed an impossible dream as my personal values were still very tied up with being a fit and active person, rather than the person living with pain that I actually was.

I learnt that through consistent mindfulness training it was possible to very gradually align my dreams and hopes with life as it is. It's work in progress and probably always will be, but I take heart from the fact that, on the whole, the things I want to do with my life are beneficial rather than harmful to my body these days. I no longer even want to climb mountains. Letting go of that dream seemed completely impossible twenty years ago and yet imperceptibly it's been replaced by a love of meditation – being an explorer of the inner world rather than the outer one. These days I have more meaning and fulfilment in my life than ever and it is sustainable within the body that I have, rather than in spite of it.

You may well find that your goals and aspirations change quite naturally as you practise mindfulness and become more self-aware. You might also find it helpful to do the 'drainers and sustainers' exercise on the following page to help you recognise more clearly what is most important to you in your life. It's also important to listen to your inner voice and follow sources of inspiration that emerge. You may decide to change your career or take up a hobby. You may realize how you've squeezed pleasurable activities out of your life and decide to go back to old interests. It doesn't matter what it is; the important thing is to find the courage to follow your heart and your dreams in a way that is aligned and integrated with your physical condition.

How to recognise your values
Before engaging in the details of the Breathworks Mindfulness in Daily Life – or pacing – Programme, it can help to spend some time connecting with your deepest values and motivations – the things that make your life worth living. This will help you clarify **why** you want to

manage your condition better, and then the details of the Breathworks pacing programme in the rest of this booklet will show you **how** to achieve this.

Sustainers and drainers

Take a blank piece of paper and list all the things in your life that sustain you and give you pleasure and energy. See if you can write your list in a free and spontaneous way jotting down whatever pops into your mind. It might be things like: friendship, playing with your children or grand-children, reading, cooking elaborate meals, listening to music, swimming.

Now take another piece of paper and write down all the things that drain you. This might be things like: dealing with authorities, driving long distances, working on the computer, talking on the telephone.

Remember that the activities I have suggested are simply theoretical examples of the sort of things to write down. You may find talking on the telephone is a sustainer, or cooking a meal is draining. Try to be as honest as you can.

Now take your list of sustainers and see if your ability to engage with these activities is impaired by your health condition. If this is the case, is there some other way you could engage with this activity so you can still enjoy these sustaining activities? For example, you may have written down that it is sustaining and satisfying to cook elaborate meals for your friends and family, but you can't do this anymore due to your back pain. If you found another way to cook, perhaps taking regular breaks throughout the process of cooking (using a paced approach as suggested in this booklet) or using some pre-cooked ingredients, do you think you could find a way back to cooking again? It is interesting to recognise that very few activities are as 'all or nothing' as we think they are. If there is a sustainer that is out of the question for you now, such as my example of climbing mountains, can you think of another way to stimulate the feelings of satisfaction and pleasure? I found it interesting to discover that meditation has given me similar feelings of excitement and adventure – but this time of the inner world. Maybe with some creative thought you can find a way to express these deep motivations and values. Let your imagination roam and see what you can come up with.

Alice

Becoming aware of what sustains me has helped me re-connect with my desire to welcome friends spontaneously into my home in a way that I've not been able to for years due to pain and fatigue. Once I remembered and recognised how up-lifting and energising I found it when friends 'popped by', I felt much more enthusiastic about engaging with paced exercise on my exercise bicycle to improve my strength, fitness and stamina to work towards that goal. Previously I'd tried exercising simply because my physiotherapist told me to and I'd not been able to find the motivation to continue it for any length of time – always giving up with a sense of failure and disappointment after a few days.

Now take a look at your list of activities that drain you. Are there ways to reduce the impact of these activities on your life? Obviously there will be activities you can't simply drop from your life as you will have responsibilities, but there may be ways to engage with these activities in a way that is less draining. For example if driving long distances is exhausting, why not break your journeys up into manageable chunks – perhaps taking a fifteen-minute break every hour? Or if you find it tiring talking on the phone, perhaps you could decide to only answer calls in the afternoons, or whatever is appropriate to your circumstances.

Now look over your lists of sustainers and drainers and see if you can identify the five most important sustaining activities to you and the five most draining activities. These are the ones to pay most attention to as you bring mindfulness into your daily life. The sustainers are the activities it is most important to prioritise and the drainers are the activities that are the most important for you to watch out for – to make sure they don't start to dominate your days.

Finally, take a piece of card small enough to carry in your purse or wallet along with your credit cards and write the five sustainers down on the card as neatly as you can. Carry this with you and when you start to feel down or uninspired take the list out and remind yourself what it is that you find enjoyable and energising in life. See if there is something you can do to connect with that ideal in the circumstances you find yourself in.

The rest of this booklet is designed to increase the impact 'sustainers' have on your life and reduce the impact of 'drainers'. By bringing mindfulness and choice into the details of your daily life you can increasingly live in a way that is rich in meaning and satisfaction for you.

The 'boom-and-bust' cycle

The first thing to do is look at some basic tendencies and begin to overcome unhelpful habits.

On our courses I ask participants to raise their hands if they have a tendency to overdo it when they feel good and then suffer deterioration in their symptoms as a consequence. Invariably, nearly everyone in the class puts their hand up. Relief fills people's faces when they see how common it is to behave in this way, even though it's destructive and self-defeating. The terms used in pain management to describe this swing from one extreme to the other are the 'over activity–under activity cycle', and 'boom and bust'.

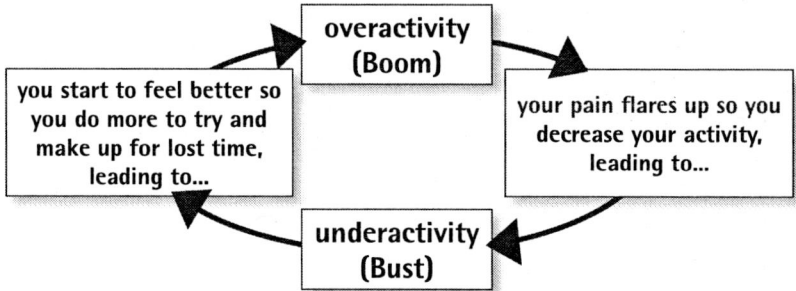

overactivity (Boom) → your pain flares up so you decrease your activity, leading to... → underactivity (Bust) → you start to feel better so you do more to try and make up for lost time, leading to... → overactivity (Boom)

The general pattern for most people living in pain is to decrease activities when the pain is bad, possibly taking to bed. Then when they have a good patch they try to all the things they haven't been able to get on with and end up over-doing it. You lose fitness while resting, so you're more likely to strain the body when you become active, and this leads to more pain. Over time flare-ups can increase and fitness deteriorate, and on top of that you feel fear, anxiety and frustration. This cycle can repeat itself many times a day, or it may play itself out over days or weeks.

You can also find yourself stuck in tendencies of fear and avoidance. Because you're frightened of doing anything that causes pain, you avoid such activities, perhaps avoiding virtually any activity. Each time you try to get back on your feet the pain and fear are even worse, so you decrease your activity further. Before long your life can be extremely limited. You hate your condition, which seems to dominate your life and you can feel like you've lost control. I know how frightening the resulting sense of powerlessness can be.

Caroline

Five years ago I was lying in bed thinking, 'This is it. This is my life. I can't do anything because my of back pain.' I dreaded the mornings, knowing I was in for another struggle. I couldn't sit or walk for long and I ended up going back to bed because the pain would ease, and I felt safe there.

Breaking the cycle

If you are to live well with your condition it's vital to break out of this cycle and restore a stable and sustainable level of activity to maintain your general health and well being, without over-doing things. Sometimes your illness or pain will mean you have to accept limitations — for example, the paralysis affecting my lower limbs means I can't walk and run as I used to. But you can still find your maximum level of activity given those limitations, and keep it as regular and varied as you can. You don't need to run a marathon — you can achieve a lot by keeping the body mobile in daily life and getting some cardiovascular exercise like swimming or faster walking to raise the heartbeat. In times of acute flare-up you may need to have time in bed, but keep it as brief as possible and return to normal daily activity as quickly as you can.
(See benefits of daily exercise in appendix 1.)

YOU decide how you live, not your pain or your feelings

People get caught in the boom/bust cycle by giving too much weight to passing feelings: overdoing things if you feel good because you have less pain, and giving up when you feel bad because you have more pain. The solution lies is in not being so driven by how you feel — your perceptions of pain, and the feelings and ideas you have about it — and acting from a broader perspective that includes your vision for your life and your realistic aspirations.

This is where mindfulness can help. In each moment you learn to rest your awareness in the body and bring objectivity to your perceptions. You can gradually peel away the layers of distorted thinking about your experience and reactive feelings like fear, anxiety, panic and despair, and rest with simple sensations as they're experienced in the body. The body scan meditation is particularly effective, and I recommend doing it each day to interrupt the boom-and-bust cycle.* Gradually you learn to accept the pain that you feel in this moment without denying it or being overwhelmed, and to be sensitive to all the other dimensions to the moment as well, including the pleasant things and your overall sense of purpose. As you're kinder to yourself, you are also more able to appreciate other people and the world.

Pacing or 'rhythm'
A cornerstone of mindfulness in daily life for people with pain and illness is learning to pace your activities. This approach is widely used within cognitive behavioural approaches to pain management and expert patient programmes. It's essential if you're to break out of the over-activity/under-activity cycle as it helps you to develop a more regular and sustainable rhythm to your days.

---

*see **www.breathworks-mindfulness.co.uk**

Betty

I love pacing when it's going well. I don't always want to do it and find it frustrating, but it has made a great transformation in my life. It has given me possibilities that I didn't know I had such as going out in the evening if I have rested. It's the concept of resting in advance of being tired that was important for me to understand. I am used to pushing myself until I'm forced into the ground, so it was new for me stop before I was exhausted, and then move onto the next activity fresh, rather than having to do it when I was already worn out. It is a complete turnaround from the way I would normally do things. I feel it's given me a huge amount of extra energy and life.

Four steps to pacing[4]

Present moment awareness

Present moment awareness means being aware of what you're doing while you're doing it, noticing how your body feels, and the thoughts and emotions that you experience. It means being awake rather than finding yourself doing something without having made a conscious decision to do it – a common tendency for many of us.

Prioritising

Once you're more aware of yourself you can make decisions about what you want to do and establish priorities. We often stumble through the day from one activity to the next without deciding what's most important; but using up precious energy doing something that isn't important can mean that you have to abandon what you really want to do. Prioritising can help you use your time and energy more effectively and lessen the risk of falling into boom and bust.

Planning

Once you've established your priorities, you need to plan what to do and how to do it before you begin. This protects you from the temptation to carry on in a fit of enthusiasm. If you need to clean your house once a week you may keep trying to do it all in one day, leading to a flare-up of your symptoms. With planning you could decide to break up the housework into sections and decide on which day you'll do each task. You can apply this to shopping, cooking, working, exercise and so on. Jenny, a long term back pain sufferer, compares the need to plan when living in pain to the need to plan your eating:

Jenny

We're used to spreading eating through the day, even though that sometimes needs planning. If we don't get that right we'll experience lack of concentration and feel ill and bad-tempered, and the hunger starts to dominate. We accept the limitations that hunger places on our lives. In the same way, I've accepted the need to plan and pace my life, as part of accepting the reality of having a body in constant pain.

Pacing or 'mindfulness rhythm'

Pacing means developing a new approach to daily life that removes the 'all or nothing' attitude and splits activities into manageable chunks. It's easy to think, 'I'll keep going and finish the job today, there's not much more to do; in any case my pain might be bad tomorrow.' This attitude is understandable, but it's short-sighted. Taking breaks today will help you function tomorrow and achieve much more in the long term.

In writing this booklet I've only worked at my computer for twenty minutes at a time, because that's how long I can work before my pain increases. Then I lie down for fifteen minutes or gently potter before returning to my computer for another twenty minutes. In this way I can work for hours at a time, whereas if I were to do what I felt like I would work until the pain became unbearable — maybe an hour or two — and then be in a bad way for the rest of the day. I get frustrated at having to take breaks, but without them I would achieve far less. It's taking me longer to write the booklet than it would take an able-bodied person, but I'm surprised how much I can achieve with this steady and regular approach.

The Breathworks Mindfulness in Daily Life (Pacing) Programme

At Breathworks we have devised a simple yet systematic method for bringing mindfulness into daily life with pacing. It involves three steps:
- Firstly you keep a diary of everything you do for seven days, noting the duration of each activity and its effect on your pain or other symptoms.
- Then you analyse the diary and work out how long you can do each activity without causing your pain or symp-

toms to increase. These are called your *baselines* and you can use a timer to stick to them.

- Later on you can gradually increase your baselines to improve fitness, stamina and quality of life without tipping into the boom-and-bust cycle.

Keeping a diary

Learning to pace is like being a detective. First you need to find out how you spend your time and which activities tend to aggravate your condition, which ease it and which don't affect your condition one way or the other.

This means keeping a diary of all your activities for seven days. Try to choose an average week so you get a clear record of how you tend to use your time. You can photocopy the template at the end of this booklet and use it for each day.

Note the time each activity takes, and your pain levels at the end. Use a scale where 0 = no pain and 10 = the worst pain imaginable. In the right hand column note whether the pain is made worse (+), eased (-), or unaffected by the activity (0). Also note rest periods (R). There's also a column for tension, by which I mainly mean muscle tension. It can help to see any connection between tension and other symptoms and even how mental or emotional tension manifests physically in the body.

Fill in this diary meticulously for seven days, but remember that its purpose is to help you think about your life. So use column headings that will be most helpful. If you're working with stress, anxiety, depression or fatigue rather than pain, then adapt the diary to track that condition.

Mindfulness of daily activity diary example sheet[5]

date	25th April				0 (no chg in pain) + (inc in pain) - (dec in pain) R (rest)
time	activity	time taken	pain at end (1-10)	tension at end (1-10)	
10.50-11.50	Packed videos and generally stressed	1 hr	7	7	+
-12.20	Relaxation tape	30'	6	5	-
-1.10	Meditation	50'	6	5	0
- 1.50	Lunch - sit up	40'	6	6	0
- 2.40	Drove Val to shops	50'	7	8	+
- 4.00	Rest	1 hr 40'	5	5	R
- 6.00	Potter at desk	2 hrs	6	7	+
- 7.00	Dinner - sit up	1 hr	6	7	0
- 8.25	Drive and get video	1 hr 25'	7	7	+
- 10.15	Lie on floor and watch video	2 hrs	6	5	-

Mindfulness of daily activity diary example sheet

date 26ᵗʰ April					0 (no chg in pain) + (inc in pain) - (dec in pain) R (rest)
time	activity	time taken	pain at end (1-10)	tension at end (1-10)	
8.25 - 8.50	Meditate - sitting up	25'	7	6	
-9.05	Continue meditating - lying down	15'	6	5	-
-9.25	Continue meditating - sitting	20'	7	6	+
-9.45	Shower and dress	20'	7	7	0
-10.45	Breakfast - sit at table	1 hr	7	7	0
-11.30	Lie on bed and read	45'	6	5	-(R)
-12.15	Sleep	45'	5	5	R
-1.00	Lie on bed and read	45'	5	5	0(R)
-1.45	Sit up for lunch	45'	7	6	+
-5.00	Lie on bed and read	3hr 15'	5	5	-(R)
-5.30	Sit up for supper	30'	6	6	+
-6.30	Go to meeting - drive myself	1hr	7	7	+
-9.45	Lie down in meeting	3hr 15'	6	6	-
-11.00	Sit in car to come home (not driving myself)	1hr 15'	8	8	+

Mindfulness of daily activity diary example sheet

date	27ᵗʰ April				0 (no chg in pain) + (inc in pain) − (dec in pain) R (rest)
time	activity	time taken	pain at end (1-10)	tension at end (1-10)	
8.30 -8.40	Few stretching exercises	10'	6	6	
-9.20	Meditate - sitting up (too long!)	40'	7	7	+
-10.10	Breakfast - lying down	50'	5	6	−
-10.50	Phone Mum - sitting up	40'	6	6	+
-12.00	Sit and do some work at desk	1hr 10'	7	7	+
-12.50	Go for swim and bit of shopping	50'	8	7	+
-1.45	Lunch - lying down	55'	5	5	−
-6.45	Lie down on bed and read	5 hrs	5	5	0 (R)
-8.15	Supper - sitting up	1 hr 30'	6	6	+
-8.30	Take a bath	15'	6	6	0
-9.15	Rest on bed	45'	5	5	R
-10.10	Potter in room	55'	7	7	+

Analysing your diary

Having completed the diary sheets for seven days, the next step is to transfer the information into three columns. In the '+' column put activities that caused extra pain (or whatever symptom you decided to monitor). In the '0' column put activities that didn't make any difference, and in the '-' column put activities that reduced your pain or symptoms. Note the times as well.

This analysis can immediately reveal patterns of which you may have been only dimly aware. In my own example sheet it's clear that sitting aggravates my condition and lying down eases it. The diary analysis showed me that I needed to pace my sitting to avoid flare-ups. Sometimes people see that they never take breaks, and run out of space on the diary sheet! This alone may explain why they're tired or can't sleep at night. Seeing this in black and white can make it easier to change your behaviour.

For example, Steve is a schoolteacher who suffers from back pain. It wasn't till he analysed his activities that he discovered that wiping the blackboard was what caused his pain. When he stopped doing that his pain was relieved. Your diary analysis may reveal something obvious like this that immediately improves your condition.

Diary analysis example sheet

DIARY EXTRACT (from one whole week's diaries)		
+ (extra pain)	**0** (no great change from 'normal' pain)	**−** (reduced pain)
Packing videos (1 hr)	Meditation (50')	Relaxation tape (30')
Drove to shop (50')	Lunch - sit up (40')	Lie on floor to watch video (2 hrs)
Potter at desk (2 hrs)	Dinner - sit up (1 hr)	Meditate - lying down (15')
Drove & get video (1 hr 25')	Shower and dress (20')	Lie on bed and read (30')
Meditate - sitting (25')	Breakfast - sit (1 hr)	Lie on bed & talk to friend (30')
MEDITATE - SIT (20')	Get dressed (10')	Lie down for breakfast (50')
Swim and shopping (30')	Lie down in meeting (3 hr)	Lie down for lunch (55')
Lunch - sit (45')	Drive to shops (20')	Lie down in Meeting (3 hrs 15')
Supper - sit (30')	Breakfast in bed (60')	Lie down and read (3hr 15')
Drive to meeting (1 hr)	Shower and dress (20')	Lie down and read (45')
Sit in car from meeting (1 hr 15')	Potter in room (30')	Lie down for breakfast (30')
Meditate - sitting (40')	Sit and talk on phone (40')	Lunch and rest (3 hrs)
Sit and talk on phone (40')	Lie on bed and read (5 hr)	
Sit at desk (1 hr 10')	Take a bath (15')	
Potter about in room (55')	Lie on bed and read (45')	
Sit to meditate (40')		
BREAKFAST - SIT (20')		
LUNCH - SIT (20')		
Work at desk (1 hr)		**Baseline sit =**
Sit at desk (30')		**20 mins x 80% =**
Potter in room (1 hr)		**16 mins**
Supper - sit (1 hr 30')		

It's also helpful to note rest periods. This shows if you're resting more on some days than on others, and you may want to even out your rest time. For example, I saw from my rest period analysis that I was lying down much more on some days than others and that I would benefit from shorter, more regular rests.

Rest period analysis example sheet

date	length (mins/hours)	total number	total time
25TH April	1 hr 40'	1	1 hr 40'
26th April	45', 45', 45', 3 hrs 15'	4	5 hrs 30'
27th April	3 hrs 45'	2	5 hrs 45'
	(You can see from my example that my rest periods are very unbalanced over the 3 days. Subsequently I tried to even them out on the basis of having discovered this through keeping the diary.)		

Establishing baselines

Having analysed your diary findings you're ready to establish baselines — the level at which you can do an activity *without causing an increase in pain* (or whatever symptoms you're monitoring). Your symptoms vary from day to day, but by setting a baseline you can establish a consistent and steady pace that won't exacerbate them.

To establish a baseline you need to look at the '+' column in the diary analysis sheet, which lists activities that caused your symptoms to increase. Identify the shortest time you spent on each activity in the week of your diary keeping. That shows that even this period of time can be too long. On my example sheet the minimum time I sat that produced an increase in pain was twenty minutes. The baseline is eighty percent of this minimum figure, which makes my sitting baseline sixteen minutes. In time you can increase your baseline as your tolerance increases, but you should start at eighty percent.

My example analysis sheet also shows that another time I sat for an hour without an increase of pain, but in finding a safe baseline you pick the shortest time that sometimes makes your condition worse, even if it doesn't always do so. This isn't an exact science — the data in my sheet doesn't tell me what would have happened to my pain levels if I'd sat for less than twenty minutes. But it's enough to set a preliminary baseline that can be fine-tuned once you put it into practice.

Having established the baseline, a timer can help you stick to it. I set the timer each time I sit down at my computer or in a meeting, and when it goes off I move and stretch my back, either by standing or lying down.

If experience shows that your baseline is too long or too short, then adjust it until you find the right level. If you want to improve your tolerances — your ability to do a certain task or activity — then you can gradually increase your baselines.

It helps to monitor one activity at a time when deciding baselines. I started with sitting, as it was obvious from my diary analysis that this was particularly problematic and that finding the time I could sit without causing flare-ups would help me to get out of my boom-and-bust cycle. Later I set baselines for other activities

Baseline record example sheet

BASELINE RECORD: *swimming* (example sheet 3)		
Baseline Level: - *swim 10 lengths in freestyle and backstroke (alternating) @ 3 times per week* *Also do leg exercises at side.*		
date	level achieved	notes
25.06.01	10 lengths in morning	Good. Exercises at side - 10 each leg - back/forward/side. Leg lifts 10 x each leg. Leg cross over exercise at deep end x 10. (Flared up later, so do less next time.)
28.06.01	10 lengths in evening	Good. Reduced leg exercise to 5 times each leg. Leg lifts 5 x each leg. Leg cross over exercise at deep end x 5. (Still flared up later but not so bad.)
30.06.01	10 lengths in morning	Good. Did the same exercises as 28.06.01 but decided to leave out the leg cross over exercise at the deep end and didn't flare up later.

and as I gradually brought greater balance to my life, I slowly became fitter. My swimming baseline chart above shows how to monitor the progress of each activity.

It's important to develop a pacing programme that works for you. These notes are guidelines, so don't be literal or mechanical. It's your life and you can be creative, within your own conditions.

Pacing can be hard. You'll often feel you're failing, but don't lose heart! I'm far from perfect at pacing myself, but I'm much,

much better than I used to be. It's important to honour your achievements and focus on your victories. Living with pain or illness is difficult and it takes a lot of patience and kindness to bring awareness and dignity back in to daily life. Remember, a pacing programme is a tool to help us – not to beat ourselves up with.

Jenny

I worked out that I could stand for about ten minutes without an increase in pain. If I'm washing up I set the timer for ten minutes and when it goes off I do something else, maybe lying down, or sitting down for several minutes. Then I do another ten minutes of washing up. It was a revelation! It had never crossed my mind to do that. I had an assumption that once you started washing-up you carried on until you'd finished. It was a revolutionary concept that you could stop doing something many times, and then start it again.

I quickly learned I'd been the drawing wrong conclusions about the increases or decreases in my pain. I knew lying down often made it feel better so I thought I should lie down for as much time as possible. I'd also noticed that going for a walk was sometimes beneficial; so I concluded that I should go for long walks. Neither strategy was helpful and I needed to learn that what I needed was frequent changes of activity. A fifteen minute walk and a ten minute lie down were best, and any more lying down produced more pain.

This immediately gave me a sense, of having a choice in dealing with pain rather than being a victim. I can't control all my external conditions, but I can be more conscious of the choices I make.

As your activity levels increase you can become fitter, enjoy life more and regain lost confidence. Pain and illness may remain a major part of your life, but they no longer control it. You do.

Three-Minute Breathing Space

Another excellent way to bring mindfulness into everyday life is through the 'three-minute breathing space'. This is simply a pause in activity, where you stop doing everything and simply 'be', resting quietly for three minutes. You can sit quietly in a comfortable position, of if you prefer, you can stand, lie down, or adopt another posture of your choice. It is a very good way of becoming more aware of what you are doing, how you are feeling, etc. and can be inserted into your activities throughout the day at regular intervals e.g. once every hour.

The first thing to do is stop what you are doing and be still, perhaps with your eyes closed (or half-closed). You can ask yourself "how do I feel in the body at this moment?" and gradually allow yourself to become more aware of the various physical sensations in the body.

You can then allow yourself to experience the gentle movements of the body as you breathe. Where there is physical pain in the body you can take your attention to that area with a kindly attitude and try to let any muscles that have tightened around the pain soften on the in and the out breath.

You can also become aware of what you are feeling emotionally and even what sort of thoughts are passing through you mind.

If you remain aware in this way of the breathing as well as any sensations, feelings and thoughts for at least three minutes you will probably find you become more 'centred'. You will then feel

> **Janet**
>
> *I find stopping very difficult. A three-minute meditation is useful in breaking up the frenzy that so quickly builds up for me in daily life. Remembering to do it can be a problem so I have learned to set a timer that goes off on the hour to remind myself: it's time to stop. I go and sit quietly for three minutes and bring my awareness back to my breath and my body and soon feel much calmer again. It is such a simple and powerful way of bringing meditation and awareness into daily life.*

more able to return to whatever activities you were engaged in with a calmer, more grounded, fresh perspective. You may find it a helpful way to interrupt any tendencies to operate from 'auto-pilot' and you may find you are able to re-gain the initiative in how you approach your activities throughout the day.

You can use a timer to remind yourself to stop at regular intervals and to time the three minutes of the breathing space.

A led version of the three minute breathing space is available for free download on **www.breathworks-mindfulness.co.uk** as one of the audio tracks that accompany the book *Living well with Pain and Illness*.

Mindfulness of Eating and Sleeping

Sometimes when we are trying to live well with pain and illness we overlook the obvious things like eating well and establishing a regular routine with sleep. No amount of meditation practice will make up for three good meals a day and periods of restorative sleep, so it is important to pay attention to these areas as well if you are to establish a helpful mindfulness in daily life practice. Pain and illness often leads to loss of career and any sense of structure to the day and it's easy to slip into chaotic routines. Health problems can also be very disruptive to sleep, so you may find yourself staying up very late and then feeling continually exhausted and sleepy during the day. When you do eventually drag yourself out of bed the first thing you do is take medication, which makes you feel nauseous as you are taking it on an empty stomach. Because you feel sick you don't do your mindful stretches or meditate and before you know it you are in a downwards slide towards poor diet, lack of exercise, and lack of motivation to meditate. You might even find yourself in a position where you never eat a proper nourishing meal. If this is true for

Sally

Sally had injured the nerves in her arm in a horrific motorcycle accident. She suffered appalling nerve pain and when she came on a Breathworks course she had not been able to lie down to sleep for years since the accident. She was on heavy medication and had lost any sense of routine: watching television during the day, staying up at night and feeling continually exhausted, snatching what sleep she could while sitting in a chair. She started practising mindfulness and incorporated regular meals into her day, including breakfast, which she hadn't eaten for years. She slowly established a sense of routine which included regular meditation and she started to feel much better. By attending to these basic daily routines she felt in charge of her life again for the first time since the accident.

you then see if you can re-establish routines, making sure you eat breakfast before you take your tablets and trying to sleep at night rather than during the day. It might take time to get yourself back on track but you will feel great rewards when you do. Seek advice from a professional if you feel you need help and advice on either diet or sleep.

Issues in Mindfulness of Daily Life

Aren't planning and pacing boring and restrictive?

When we introduce the pacing or 'mindfulness rhythm' module on the Breathworks course people often think, 'Oh dear, has my life really come to this? What about spontaneity and fun?' The strongest reply I can think of is my own experience. I'm a naturally impulsive, driven person and when I first encountered the idea of pacing it sounded awful. I kept on living in boom-and-bust for years, having flare-ups and occasionally serious relapses that would send me to bed for months at a time. Eventually I realised that I needed to take myself in hand. I got books about pacing and made a real effort to change my habits, but I still didn't make much headway. I thought I was a hopeless case. Only when I started teaching the Breathworks programme did I finally made the right effort and reap the benefits. I applied it initially to sitting at my desk, then to swimming and before long I realised how valuable it was as an approach to life. I'm now a convert, and I think that if I can pace, then anyone can. Because pacing means that my energy is more stable and balanced I can make social engagements more reliably than in my un-paced days, and be more spontaneous within them. That's why I like to describe pacing as establishing a mindfulness rhythm. It is very rewarding to find a

Maria

I really value taking one moment at a time and not trying to live the next 12 hours in advance. I have tended to live by so many lists that I'd grind myself to a total halt. I'm learning the wisdom of just doing one or two things each day, taking my time over them, valuing them and making wise choices about prioritising. Yes, it means some things have had to go, but guess what? I don't miss them because I am enjoying what I do more.

rhythm to one's activities that is sustainable and reliable rather than lurching from boom to bust.

The need for acceptance

It's hard to engage with pacing if you haven't, at least to come extent, accepted the reality of your situation. Resistance to pacing is often tied up with a fantasy of going back to being youthful, energetic and pain-free. But eventually you need to accept the new reality. This may mean that you need to grieve for the mobility, health or energy you've lost before being able to connect with a deeper motivation for changing the way you behave in daily life that is more aligned with your condition. Being blunt, you could say that you have two options: either you pace and make the most of your situation, or you don't pace and stay trapped in the boom/bust cycle. Trying to live out a fantasy existence will only lead to sorrow.

Doing your best

Nobody paces perfectly. You can only do your best in the knowledge that every bit of awareness helps. Habits die hard and you aren't going to change them overnight, so you need kindness and patience.

Mindfulness of daily life is an art, like music or sculpture, which means constantly responding to circumstances as you work with the raw material of your life, and adapting in a flowing and gentle way.

Diane

Awareness can mean different things to each of us. Sometimes it means being aware of your needs. When I first experienced vertigo — not on a cliff top but in my living room — I thought I'd never write or study again. I could no longer work for hours without a break. Now I've learned to work for short, timed sessions and use a sloping desk for writing. These aids help me write and study as long as I remain mindful. I even managed to take exams once my needs were clear.

Pacing in public

Pacing when you're with others takes confidence. It's one thing to use a timer at home, but something else to stand up or lie down in a public place or a meeting. But it can be done, and people are usually surprisingly supportive if you explain your needs in a straightforward way. Be patient with yourself if you don't always manage that: it isn't easy. I still find it difficult to stand out from the crowd in this kind of way, despite years of practice.

Mary, who has longstanding back pain has a senior post as an education advisor and often gives talks to hundreds of people. She has no problems with this, but asking for a chair so she could sit down during her presentation provoked enormous anxiety, even though standing caused her considerable pain.

Activities you can't leave or think you can't pace

Often people think they can't pace at work because of pressures from the task, colleagues or management. If this is the case you'll need to find subtle ways to pace that aren't obvious to others. For example, if you need to move around regularly to manage your health condition you can go for regular drinks of water, or take regular toilet breaks. You might stand and stretch when you reach your baseline tolerance, or move files around on the desk or walk to another part of the room. If you want to avoid the disruption of using a timer you could use the vibrate alert on a mobile phone, or a clock with a quiet beep.

People often feel they can't pace when they're bringing up small children or doing caring work in the family. There are plenty of ways to be imaginative here, as well. What's important is bringing awareness to daily life and avoiding unhelpful behaviour. If working to baselines is difficult you can still bring awareness to how you move your body and how you use the time when the person you're caring for is sleeping or resting. You might be able to do some stretches or a short body scan, or whatever is helpful for maintaining mindfulness and initiative.

Pacing with a degenerative condition

If you have a degenerative condition you may find that your baselines and tolerances decrease over time. It's important to incorporate this in to your pacing awareness, so you don't feel you're failing. Richard, a man in his early fifties with progressive multiple sclerosis, really liked the idea of pacing and trying to maintain function, but found he couldn't maintain his baselines over time. At first he felt despondent, but I encouraged him to focus on practices he could do, such as the body scan, no matter how severe

> **Bill**
>
> *Bill suffered from back pain and was recovering from a stroke, while both his parents were in their nineties and his father had severe dementia. When he was pushing his father around in his wheelchair, he'd stop every ten minutes when his timer went off and say 'Look, Pops, look at the view over there.' Having a proper break and becoming more aware of himself and his surroundings enabled him to soften his response to his neck and back pain. That helped him to be more caring towards his father and to cope with the stresses in his life with more equanimity.*

his symptoms were. I also encouraged him to maintain baselines as well as he could, allowing for a decrease over time, to avoid falling back into the boom/bust cycle. He continued to attend day retreats and drop-in classes for several years as he managed his illness with as much awareness as possible. His gentle acceptance and quiet determination to make the most of his life always had a positive effect on the group.

Sometimes pacing means doing more, not less

We generally tend to think of pacing in terms of reducing the length of time we do an activity so we don't get into over-drive and 'boom', which will then lead to 'bust' or exhaustion. However, sometimes people discover that they need to do *more* of an activity in order to maintain a healthy mindfulness rhythm and maintain their well-being.

> **Steve**
>
> *Steve has diabetic peripheral neuropathy that causes pain in his feet. When he investigated mindfulness in daily life through diary keeping, he discovered that a daily walk of two hours was far more effective for his pain levels and blood sugar management, than a walk of just 30 minutes. So, for him, establishing pacing or mindfulness rhythm meant he needed to extend his daily walk, rather than break it up into manageable chunks as he had expected. He also had to make changes to his lifestyle so he could make a long walk a regular activity, sustained over time.*

Do something enjoyable in rest periods

You are more likely to keep to pacing if you intersperse the activities you're pacing with an enjoyable, relaxing activity. For example, if you need to lie down regularly but find it hard to stop, you may find that reading a good book or magazine will help you keep to your pacing plans. If you don't enjoy your 'breaks' then you'll get frustrated and be more likely to keep going with activities when you need to stop.

Diane was a great fan of a TV drama called 'The Sopranos'. She would do some housework for a timed period and then take a break and watch ten minutes of a Sopranos DVD before getting back to work.

In my own mindfulness rhythm of twenty minutes on the computer interspersed with fifteen minutes lying down, I've learned that I'm happiest when I read an undemanding novel with a good plot when I rest. Thrillers seem to fit the bill particularly well! I can easily re-engage with my 'resting' activity and I don't feel as frustrated.

Sometimes of course I want to hurl the timer across the room and ignore it when it's telling me to stop working, and sometimes I do. I can lose my awareness and push on for longer than twenty minutes. But I always pay the price in increased symptoms, so I've gradually accepted that pacing is really the only sustainable way to maintain a good quality of life when living with pain.

Summary

- Remember, pacing is taking a break *before* you need it. That's the key to maintaining mindfulness and interrupting the over activity/under activity cycle.
- Start within your baselines, doing only what you're sure you can manage, and gradually increase the amount you do or the time you spend on it. Be ready to leave for now activities that are too hard. You can come back to them as you get fitter. Starting with activities that are easier will bring confidence.
- By establishing baselines, you will learn to make better judgments about activity, position change and rest. Remember to change your position regularly. For example, while preparing a meal, try alternating between standing and sitting, as well as taking a short rest break every now and then.
- Vary the ways you use your body throughout the day, making sure that you use different muscle groups. For example, don't try to do all your vacuuming in one day but spread it over the week. Vary your activities between sitting, walking, standing and lying.

- Keep to your targets and plans as much as you can without being obsessive or rigid. USE YOUR TIMER!

- This will mean that you, not your pain or illness, will decide how much you do. On a bad day, try to keep going as planned but pace yourself more, taking more rest breaks. On a good day, be careful not to do more than you've planned. Avoid overdoing things.

- Following these guidelines, you should have fewer pain flare-ups, gradually find yourself doing more and regain a sense of initiative and confidence.

Appendix 1

Physical consequences of reduced activity[6]
Inactivity affects the body remarkably quickly, with many physical consequences. If we aren't careful our pain problem will be compounded by other health difficulties associated simply with disuse.

Mindfulness in daily life can help us maintain or gradually regain mobility or physical activity which will lead to improved health and reverse the dangers of physical inactivity. Remember, bodies are designed to move. If you don't move some of the consequences will be:

Brain: Inactivity means there is less circulation of the blood to the brain and less oxygen in the brain cells. You feel tired and sluggish and have disturbed sleep, an increased susceptibility to stress and a higher risk of depression.

Muscles and tendons: Muscles are designed to move. If they are over-rested the tissues become more fibrous, lose bulk and become more painful when stretched. Even one day of bed rest leads to a loss of eight grams of protein.

Joints: The joints may lose stability as the muscles supporting them weaken. The capsule around the joint can become tight, restricting movement.

Bone: With each week of bed rest 1.54g of calcium is lost. After six months of complete bed rest, forty percent of the body's calcium is lost. When bones lose calcium they become brittle and prone to fractures.

Cardiovascular system: Like any other muscle the heart gets smaller and works less efficiently if it isn't exercised. By pumping blood around the body the heart causes oxygen, which is essential to vitality, to be delivered to the body's cells and waste products to be excreted. When we exercise the heart-rate is raised, the lungs expand and blood vessels throughout the body become more flexible. Lack of exercise makes these systems sluggish increasing the risk of high blood pressure and fatty deposits around the heart. Red blood cells, which deliver oxygen, become smaller and less efficient and we feel more tired.

Genitourinary system: The kidneys grow smaller as the body becomes sluggish and their waste filtering system slows down. The bladder also shrinks as it doesn't need to store as much urine.

Sensory: Bed rest can lead to a reduction in sharpness of sight, hearing and taste. Balance can also be affected.

Appendix 2

Sense Awareness Inventory[7]

Another way we can become more mindful of daily life is to become more aware of subtle experiences, such as those we perceive through the senses. While most of us understand what each sense is and how it affects us, it is easy to forget the benefits of really noticing our sensory experience as it occurs and enjoying the positive emotions that arise as a consequence.

We've all enjoyed a gorgeous sunset, a spectacular view, the smell of good food, the touch of something warm and gentle, the sound of laughter or a friend's voice; but it is very easy to forget to appreciate these simple pleasures, especially when living with pain, illness and/or stress.

By engaging with all our senses in this way – what psychotherapists call 'multi-model awareness', we can learn to identify ways of acting that help to ensure our well-being in the fullest sense and protect us from harm by being awake to the world around us and in touch with pleasure.

To help us do this we can use a simple method to identify more closely our experiences using the SAI or Sense Awareness Inventory. This helps us identify the pleasure, comfort and enjoyment we get in our daily lives using each of our senses.

If you look at the chart on page 51 you'll see that you can list all the things you can think of that give pleasure with each sense organ. Then in the final column you can list all the activities that bring you pleasure, enjoyment and comfort.

Once you have completed the form you can reflect on how you can use the information in your daily life. For example, if the beauty of nature brings pleasure, you can ask yourself how often you take the time to look for it. Can you make more effort to appreciate beauty when it appears in the world around you? If it is the sound of a Bach sonata, can you make more time to listen to it? Look through the list and ask yourself how often you make time to do the activities, or appreciate the senses that give you pleasure and think about how you could prioritise these activities and experiences more. Also notice how simple (and cheap!) most of these things are. It doesn't cost anything to appreciate a sunset, the smell of cooking, or how green the grass is on a summer's day.

Photocopy the template on pg 54 and fill it in from time to time to remind you of these simple, accessible ways to bring pleasure into your life.

Sense Awareness Inventory

Under each heading please list as many items as possible (10-20) from which you get pleasure, enjoyment or comfort.

Sight	Sound	Smell	Taste	Touch	Activity
A sunset	Rain on the roof	The smell of bushes after rain	Fresh coffee	The coat of a long haired dog when it is dry	Walking in the country
Birds on the feeder	Olivia's violin music	Scones baking	Fresh cup of tea	Wind against the skin on warm summer's day	Watching a good DVD
The colour red	Chopin piano pieces	New baked bread	Mint chocolate		Reading a good novel
The green of nature after rain	Wind in the trees	Coffee grinds	Fresh orange as it bursts in the mouth	Sunlight on body	Going swimming and having Jacuzzi afterwards
The sea	Birds	Grass on a hot summer's day	Toothpaste	Furry underside of leaves	Reading newspaper in a coffee shop
Petals of a rose	Silence at night in the country	Tea tree and mint shampoo	Good red wine	Silk	Doing body scan meditation
Dogs and cats	Waves on a beach	Healing massage balm	Cool fresh water	Smooth bark of a eucalyptus tree	relaxing in a hot bath
The flowers of spring bulbs	Joni Mitchell music	A scented rose	Salted licorice	A horse's muzzle	talking to my friends
Trees	A cat purring	Smell of lilies	Lingonberry jam	Holding a baby	
Seeing loved ones	Rustle of leaves		Ben & Jerry's cherry garcia Ice cream		

Appendix 3

Diary templates for photocopying

Mindfulness of Daily Activity Diary Sheet

date time	activity	time taken	pain at end (1–10)	tension at end (1–10)	0 (no chg in pain) + (inc in pain) - (dec in pain) R (rest)

Diary Analysis Sheet (from one whole week's diaries)

+ (extra pain)	0 (no great change from 'normal' pain)	– (reduced pain)

Rest Period Analysis Sheet

REST PERIODS	length (mins/hours)	total number	total time
date			

Baseline Record Sheet

BASELINE RECORD:

Baseline Level:

date	level achieved	notes

Sensory Awareness Inventory

Sight	Sound	Smell

Under each heading please list as many items as possible (10-20) from which you get pleasure, enjoyment or comfort.

Taste	Touch	Activity

Footnotes

[1] Jon Kabat-Zinn, *Wherever You Go, There You Are: Mindfulness Meditation In Everyday Life*, Hyperion, (1994), p. 4

[2] Mark Williams, John Teasdale, Zindel Segal, Jon Kabat-Zinn, *The Mindful Way Through Depression: Freeing Yourself From Chronic Unhappiness*, The Guildford Press (2007), p. 48

[3] Ibid. p. 5

[4] Adapted from Pete Moore, *Persistent Pain Programme Handbook (PPP)*, part of the Expert Patient Programme run by the National Health Service in the UK, 2006

[5] All pacing and baseline diaries, analysis sheets and templates adapted from *Pain Relief without Drugs* by Jan Sadler, Healing Arts Press, Rochester, VT 05767 Copyright © 1997, 2001, 2007 Inner Traditions / Bear & Co. www.HealingArtsPress.com

[6] Michael Nicholas, Allan Molloy, Lois Tonkin, Lee Beetson, *Manage Your Pain*, Souvenir Press Ltd, (2003), p. 75

[7] The Sensory Awareness Inventory was pioneered by Dr. George W. Burns, clinical psychologist and Director of the Milton Erikson Institute

Vidyamala Burch

Originally from New Zealand, Vidyamala sustained a spinal injury when she was 16. Over 20 years ago she started exploring mindfulness and meditation to manage her own persistent pain and in 2001 began offering these skills to others, initially with funding from the Millennium Commission in the UK. She regularly leads meditation retreats as well as offering mindfulness training internationally to anyone wanting to ease their suffering within the context of Breathworks. In 2008 she published *Living Well with Pain and Illness: the mindful way to free yourself from suffering* which is based on the Breathworks programme.

More from breathworks:

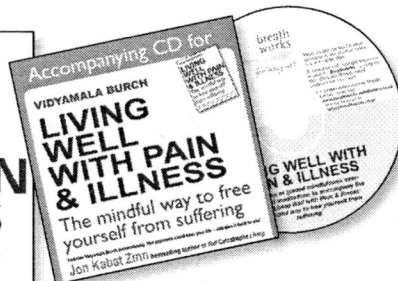

Living Well With Pain and Illness
Paperback Book 255 pages
    ISBN 978-0-7499-2860-5
1 x CD guided meditation
    ISBN 978-0-9550120-6-8

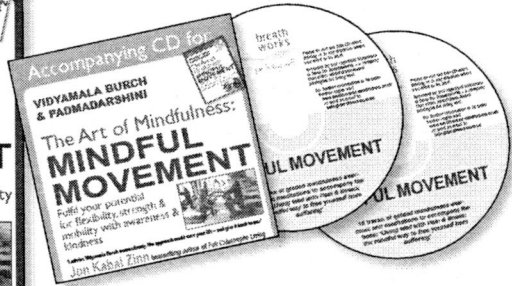

Set: "Mindful Movement"
Booklet + 2 x audio CDs
ISBN 978-0-9550120-9-9
DVD to come in 2009

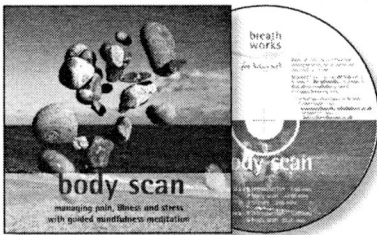

body scan
1 CD
guided meditation
ISBN 978-0-9550120-3-7

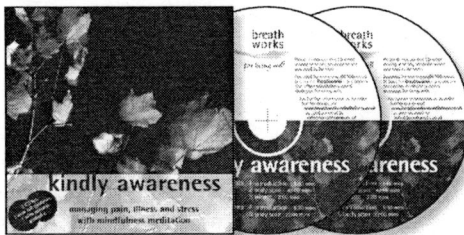

kindly awareness
2 CDs
a) guided meditation
b) minimal guidance
ISBN 978-0-9550120-5-1

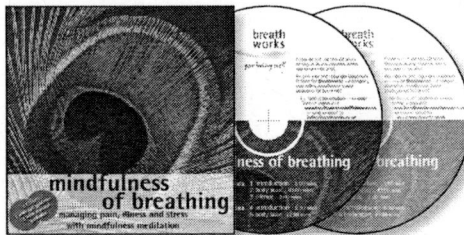

minfulness of breathing
2 CDs
a) guided meditation
b) minimal guidance
ISBN 978-0-9550120-4-4